The Elephant Keeper

To everyone who helps to protect wildlife on our planet — M.R.

Every big challenge takes one's own effort and hard work,
but also guidance, especially from those close to our hearts.
This humble effort I dedicate to my sweet and loving mother. — P.C.

◆ ◆ ◆

Kids Can Press gratefully acknowledges the financial support
of the Government of Ontario, through the Ontario Media Development
Corporation; the Ontario Arts Council; the Canada Council for the Arts; and the
Government of Canada, through the CBF, for our publishing activity.

Published in Canada and the U.S. by Kids Can Press Ltd.
25 Dockside Drive, Toronto, ON M5A 0B5

Kids Can Press is a Corus Entertainment Inc. company

www.kidscanpress.com

The artwork in this book was rendered in
mixed media painting and Photoshop.
The text is set in Remo Pro.

Edited by Yasemin Uçar
Designed by Julia Naimska

Printed and bound in Shenzhen, China,
in 3/2017 by C & C Offset

CM 17 0 9 8 7 6 5 4 3 2 1

Library and Archives Canada Cataloguing in Publication

Ruurs, Margriet, 1952–, author
The elephant keeper : caring for orphaned elephants
in Zambia / written by Margriet Ruurs ; illustrated by Pedro Covo.

(CitizenKid)
ISBN 978-1-77138-561-9 (hardback)

I. Covo, Pedro, 1988–, illustrator II. Title. III. Series: CitizenKid

PS8585.U97E44 2017   jC813'.54   C2016-906424-7

The Elephant Keeper

Caring for Orphaned Elephants in Zambia

Written by

Margriet Ruurs

Illustrated by

Pedro Covo

CitizenKid™

A collection of books that inform children about the
world and inspire them to be better global citizens

Kids Can Press

Orphaned

The sun was a glowing red ball in the eastern sky when Aaron left his family's hut. It was still dark, but he knew just where to place his bare feet on the dusty path. He walked the six kilometers between his village and Lion's Lodge twice a day.

He'd started working at the lodge just a few months ago. It had been his father's job, until he got sick. Then the manager, knowing the family needed the income, offered the job to Aaron.

He wasn't nearly as strong as his father had been before his illness, but Aaron worked hard. He carried bundles of reeds and learned to thatch roofs. He hauled lumber, handed nails to the carpenter and sharpened the ax. He fetched water from the well for the workers and did other hot jobs, such as burning debris and raking leaves.

As Aaron approached the gate, he was startled by a strange noise. Must be an animal, he thought — but he could tell right away that this wasn't just a hippo in the nearby Zambezi River. Aaron dashed through the lane of palm trees, rounded the corner and stopped dead in his tracks. He couldn't believe his eyes — a small elephant was flailing around in the lodge's swimming pool!

The elephant held its trunk in the air to avoid drowning and kicked wildly, ears flapping like sails on a boat that had sprung a leak.

Aaron glanced around nervously for the mother elephant. Was she nearby? Fear knotted in the pit of his stomach. Elephants often roamed near his village, trampling everything in their path. Hadn't they just recently killed one of the villagers?

But there were no other elephants in sight, and this one needed help — fast. Aaron raced to the cottage where the gardener slept. "Help! Hurry!" he called, pounding on the door.

What should he do? He had seen elephant mothers use their trunks to guide and prod their babies. Could he somehow guide this one to the edge?

He ran to the pool shed and flung the door open. With shaking hands, he rummaged through the equipment, grabbing a rope, a hose, a rake. When he got back, the gardener, still in his pajamas, was beside the pool. The manager came running from the lodge, followed by the cook, who had heard all the commotion. Sleepy guests appeared at their windows. Soon they, too, converged on the lawn in their pajamas, holding cameras.

Aaron threw the hose and rake down on the deck and, surprising even himself, jumped straight into the water. The little elephant snorted and splashed frantically. But it was getting tired, and this allowed Aaron to get close with the rope. One of the boys who worked in the kitchen jumped in, too. Together they were able to get the rope under the elephant's belly. With the cook and gardener pulling from the edge, Aaron and the other boy attempted to push the elephant up, doing their best to steer clear of its thrashing feet.

But it was no use.

The lodge's guests shouted encouragement. "You can do it! Keep trying! Don't let it drown!"

Aaron looked into the elephant's eyes. He saw terror there. But he also thought he glimpsed a flicker of hope. Hope that it would be saved. Aaron took a deep breath.

"On the count of three!" he yelled.

Between them, the men on the ground and the boys in the pool finally managed to drag, pull and push the exhausted animal onto the deck. Aaron climbed out of the water and sat on the edge, panting and dripping. He watched the elephant, lying on its side, trembling. It looked straight at Aaron and blinked. Aaron couldn't take his eyes off it. This was a wild elephant?

A truck pulled up and some men in uniform stepped out. He saw them waving their arms and overheard snippets of their conversation with the lodge manager: "... found the mother ... killed ... poachers ..."

Aaron wondered if animals had feelings like humans. Did it see its mother getting killed?

The men loaded the elephant into the truck. Aaron heard them talking about medical checkups and an elephant orphanage. One of the men shook his head. "Such a young elephant might not survive ..."

◆ ◆ ◆

Walking home after work, Aaron thought of the animal he had helped rescue. Never before had he touched the thick, rough skin of an elephant. He wondered if it was at the orphanage now and how it was doing. Was it still alive?

When he reached home, his mother was sitting outside their hut. She had prepared a meal of *nshima* with vegetable stew and handed a bowl to Aaron. The story of the elephant had already reached the village.

"Aaron!" a neighbor called. "Did you think we needed more of those thieving giants trampling our crops?"

Aaron's cheeks burned. He hung his head and picked at his food.

"Don't listen to them," his mother said. "You did the right thing. You don't just let an animal die."

"Even if it might kill you, or steal from you?"

His mother shrugged. "They are hungry. We are the ones who know how to grow food, so they come here. To them, it is not stealing — it is survival."

Aaron thought of how they often lost mangoes and corn to foraging elephants, and how that meant they had no crops to sell, no money to pay for the things they needed.

"I hear that in some places, people plant hedges of fiery peppers around the crops to keep elephants away," his mother added. "Killing them is not a good solution."

"But they kill people ..." Aaron said, thinking of the villager who had been trampled.

"Mutunwa was killing elephants," his mother said, as if reading his mind. "He knew that it was dangerous."

Aaron sighed. It was complicated.

How Big Is an Elephant?

At birth, healthy baby elephants weigh 60 to 90 kg (130 to 200 lb.) and stand about 1 m (3 ft.) tall. When fully grown, they can weigh 2268 to 6350 kg (5000 to 14 000 lb.) and be 4 m (13 ft.) tall. This makes an elephant about as big and heavy as a helicopter!

Adult elephants will eat some 200 to 300 kg (440 to 660 lb.) of grasses, twigs, bark and leaves each day and drink more than 160 L (42 gal.) of water!

Milk Dependency

In the wild, elephant babies are fully dependent on their mothers' milk for the first two years and continue to nurse up to five years, sometimes longer. Without the essential nutrients of their mothers' milk, orphaned elephants can be in deep trouble. At an orphanage, elephants under the age of three are bottle-fed a special, nutrient-rich formula every three hours around the clock. After that, weaning begins — the frequency of bottle feedings and the concentration of the formula are gradually reduced until the elephants can live on an adult diet.

Elephants in Danger

Illegal hunting (called "poaching"), habitat destruction and other human-elephant conflicts have caused a rapid decline in elephant populations. There is a real danger that the species could become extinct within the next fifty years.

Thousands of elephants are killed each year for their ivory tusks, often leaving orphaned babies behind. Tusks are extra-long teeth and are very useful tools elephants use to peel bark from trees and to dig for food or water to drink. They're also powerful weapons against enemies. Some people buy the ivory, even though it is illegal, and use it to make objects such as jewelry and ornaments.

A Friendship Begins

As Aaron walked to the lodge the next morning, he worried. Would he lose his job for jumping into the pool and making a spectacle of himself in front of the guests? If he lost his job, how would he manage to help his family?

As soon as he reported for work, he was told to go and see the lodge manager. His heart sank.

Aaron stood in front of the manager's desk, his eyes fixed on the ground.

"You were brave yesterday," the manager said.

Aaron looked up in surprise.

"The game rangers who collected the elephant run an orphanage not far from here. They told me that poachers forced a herd of elephants to flee last night. This little one likely got separated, and there was nothing the others could do but keep going …" He sighed. "They also told me that you can visit the little elephant, if you like."

The manager got up from his desk then and put a hand on Aaron's shoulder. "I wanted to thank you for what you did," he said, smiling. "Our guests were most impressed."

◆ ◆ ◆

A few days later, Aaron found himself walking down the long, dusty road that led to town and to the elephant orphanage. He had never thought of animals being orphans. Did it miss its mother like he missed his father? He hoped the little elephant was still alive.

When he arrived, two men were playing a game of checkers with bottle caps at the gate. One of the men recognized him and called out, "*Mwasela seyi*, Aaron!"

"Hello," Aaron answered shyly.

"Did you come to visit Zambezi?" The man smiled and held out his hand. "I am Samuel, one of the elephant keepers."

"Zambezi?"

"It's the name we gave the little elephant who went for a swim. We named him for the mighty river."

So the elephant *was* alive. Aaron grinned, his heart beating faster. Samuel motioned for him to follow.

That's when Aaron came upon a sight that he would never have believed if he hadn't seen it with his own eyes. Three grown men were chatting to each other, while elephants mingled around them. Aaron's mouth dropped open.

Samuel laughed. "It *is* possible for elephants and people to be friends," he said as he opened the door to a barn. It smelled of hay and dung. Aaron hung back, wary.

"Come, I will introduce you properly to Zambezi," said Samuel.

Zambezi lay on a bed of straw in a corner of a stall. He looked like a wrinkled bag of bones, covered by blankets. He seemed to be having trouble breathing. The image of his father, lying under blankets at home just before he died, flashed through Aaron's mind and he felt a lump in his throat.

Samuel nudged him forward. "Go on, you can touch him," he said.

Aaron knelt and, hand shaking, reached out to touch Zambezi's thick skin. It felt surprisingly warm.

Zambezi opened one eye. Slowly, his trunk curled upward and brushed Aaron's arm.

Did the elephant recognize him?

"Kanjani ...?" Aaron whispered. He sat down on the straw, and the elephant rested his trunk on Aaron's leg.

They stayed like that for some time, while Samuel watched them curiously.

"Here," Samuel whispered, handing a milk bottle to Aaron. "Maybe you will have better luck than we've had ..."

Aaron had seen enough babies nurse to know what to do. He tilted the bottle, spilling some drops onto the elephant's lip. Zambezi licked the milk off his lip then began to suck from the bottle, looking Aaron in the eyes as he did.

Samuel shook his head in amazement and tiptoed away.

Aaron was still sitting on the ground with Zambezi's head cradled in his lap when Samuel returned with the veterinarian.

The men looked from the boy to the elephant to the empty bottle, and back to Aaron.

The vet smiled. "We're going to need you to do that again," he said.

"He wouldn't drink like that when we tried," Samuel explained. "When he didn't finish his bottles, I was pretty sure he would die soon ..."

The vet gently prodded the elephant's sunken cheeks. "Bezi is not much more than a month old," he said. "He has been traumatized by losing his mother. He is also very sick from not getting his mother's milk. We've been giving him medicine and fluids to fight dehydration."

Afterward, Samuel showed Aaron around the compound.

There was a corral where other orphans played. They had a mud puddle for splashing, trees for browsing in — and two of the elephants were kicking a plastic barrel back and forth between them like a soccer ball.

Will Zambezi ever be able to play in there? Aaron wondered. It seemed unlikely.

Samuel explained that the keepers took care of the animals day and night. He showed Aaron the kitchen where bottles of special formula with vitamins and medicine were prepared.

"They are our babies," Samuel said with a smile.

The remark took Aaron by surprise, even though he could see it was true.

It was confusing. Elephants were dangerous animals. But here the keepers cared for them as if they were children.

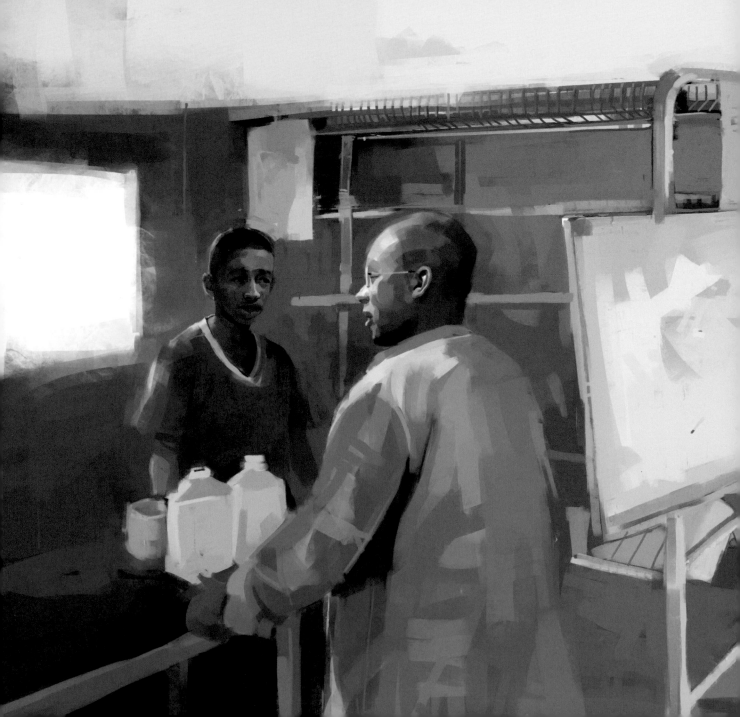

The head keeper, Gift, found them in the kitchen.
"So, you are the boy who rescued Bezi from the pool,"
he said. "Samuel tells me you are a natural caregiver."
Aaron smiled shyly.
Gift watched his face closely. "How would you like to
work here?" he asked.
Aaron stared at him, astonished. "Work here?"
"We have a shortage of keepers," Gift said. "And we have
another orphan arriving soon. You are good with animals.
Think about it. We will train you and pay you a good wage,
but you would need to live close to here. The elephants
need round-the-clock care."

On the long walk home, Aaron's thoughts tumbled through his head. What would his mother say? Would she approve of his leaving home to work at the elephant orphanage? Gift had said that the keepers sleep in the stalls with the elephants. Was he brave enough to sleep near an elephant, even a small one?

Would he make enough money to buy wire to fix the fence or the charcoal burner his mother wanted so they could cook without wood?

What would his boss at Lion's Lodge say? What would the other villagers think?

Probably that he had gone crazy.

"Your father would be proud," his mother said when he told her about the job offer. "*I* am proud of you." She took his hands in hers. "We will miss you, but we will manage. And, of course, you will come home on your days off."

Aaron grinned, because it sounded like an order.

And just like that, his decision was made.

◆ ◆ ◆

The very next day, Aaron spoke to the lodge manager, who said he was sorry to see him go, but that he also understood that the job at the orphanage was an opportunity not to be missed.

Social Bonds

Elephants are highly intelligent animals, and, like humans, they form very strong emotional and social bonds with one another. They live in herds, care for and protect one another, and show affection. Baby elephants need these social bonds as much as they need food and drink. As with humans, their memory, intelligence and social nature make elephants vulnerable to stress and trauma.

Baby elephants are often indirect victims of poaching and other human-elephant conflicts. Without a parent to teach them how, they can have problems foraging for food and socializing with other elephants. They can also suffer from post-traumatic stress, which often causes behavior problems that make it nearly impossible to integrate into a new herd.

In a herd, all females over the age of about six help to look after the babies. The oldest female is called the matriarch and she is the leader of the herd. She might be mother, grandmother, aunt or sister of the others in her group. Female elephants remain in their family group their whole lives. Young males (bulls) leave the group when they are ten to fifteen years old and live mostly alone.

In the wild, elephants live to around sixty or seventy years of age.

Daily Life of an Elephant Keeper

The keepers who look after orphaned elephants are always busy. Their duties include:

- preparing bottles of special formula and feeding them to the elephants every few hours

- cleaning stalls and supplying fresh hay

- supporting the veterinarian, who checks the animals' health and gives them any shots or medication they need

- supervising the elephants' playtime, when they learn about hierarchy and dominance. (The elephants play in mud puddles, and sometimes use "toys," such as sticks or branches.)

- taking the elephants for walks to teach how to forage for food and avoid predators, such as lions and crocodiles

- on hot days, spraying the elephants with water, and protecting them from the sun with blankets and even sunscreen. (Without its mother there to shade it, a baby elephant is at risk of sunburn.)

- taking notes and recording the elephants' feedings, behavior, temperature, bowel movements, etc.

- doing maintenance to make sure the fences surrounding the boma (animal enclosure) are secure

- putting blankets over the elephants at night and sleeping near them

- providing the elephants with the constant love and reassurance essential to their survival and well-being

- educating tourists and the local population about wildlife preservation

A New Home

The first few nights at the orphanage were not easy. Aaron hardly slept at all. With every snort Bezi gave, Aaron sat straight up, heart pounding in his chest. He missed the familiar sounds and smells of home — his sister's soft, rhythmic breathing nearby, the goats bleating ... But it wasn't long before he began to find comfort in the closeness of Bezi and the warm scent of straw.

Samuel and the other keepers showed him tricks to get Bezi to swallow pills and how to take blood for the vet to check. Bezi was still very sick, sleeping most of the day in the quiet stable. But now, at least, he drank the bottles that the keepers offered him every few hours. Aaron recorded the amounts that Bezi drank. He held his head as the vet took Bezi's temperature or administered medicine. He even recorded the elephant's bowel movements. He felt proud when Bezi finished his milk, and covered him with a blanket at night.

"I'm turning into an elephant mother," he joked to Samuel.

But mothers worry, and so did Aaron. Each time he saw the vet frown, Aaron's stomach tightened. When Bezi spat out his medicine, Aaron feared that he'd never get better. One morning, he noticed that Bezi's heartbeat was very, very slow compared to his own. Samuel reassured him that all elephants have a slower heartbeat than humans. But that didn't stop Aaron from worrying. Bezi still had a fever. Aaron knew only too well that medicine couldn't cure everything ...

One morning, Aaron watched wistfully as the other elephants played, kicking an old bucket and rolling joyfully in the mud.

If only Bezi could have the company of other elephants, he was thinking, when suddenly he heard Samuel shout, "Come quick!"

Aaron dropped the rake he was holding and ran to where Samuel and the other keepers crowded around a dusty truck. Gift lowered the tailgate, and there lay the still, gray body of a young elephant. She'd been tranquilized, and she had an ugly wound on one of her hind feet from being caught in a snare.

Gift instructed the keepers on how to best move the elephant to a stall in the barn. It took eight men to carry her on a tarp stretched between them. As they worked, Aaron found out that this elephant had even been on an airplane. Wildlife officers were able to rescue her from the bush up north, but they didn't have the resources there to look after her. Now it was up to the staff at the orphanage to keep Suni alive.

The vet sprayed her leg with disinfectant and plastered it with green clay, a natural healing remedy. Aaron ran for blankets to cover the injured elephant. He stroked her head while the vet checked her heart rate and administered antibiotics.

It wasn't until the new elephant was settled in her stall that Aaron realized with a start that he'd forgotten all about Zambezi. He had never left him alone this long before. He couldn't believe he'd been so careless! What if something had happened to him?

Aaron sprinted toward the barn.

He had been preparing himself for the worst, but he got a shock of a different kind ...

The little elephant was standing up, trunk hanging over the half wall of his stall. He seemed to be trying to reach some plastic bottles.

Aaron laughed with relief. "Bezi! Are you hungry? Are you getting into trouble now? I guess that's a good sign!" He rubbed the little elephant's trunk, and Bezi nuzzled Aaron's arm.

Unfortunately, help had come too late for Suni. Her leg was badly infected, and she died of her wounds soon after coming to the orphanage. It was a terribly sad day for all the keepers. Aaron couldn't help but notice Gift turning his back to wipe his eyes when the vet shared the news.

Bezi had been luckier and was getting better each day. His sagging skin slowly gave way to a round tummy, and his cheeks filled out, too. Before long, he was moving around more, even trying to leave his stall. The other orphans approached curiously, prodding him all over with their trunks.

Eventually, Bezi was allowed to venture outside. He adored the older orphans, following them around the corral and imitating their behavior. He watched them reach up to strip branches and chase each other, trying to steal the green leaves. Bezi's eyes sparkled as he splashed in the mud. And whenever he spotted Aaron, he came running over to search for a bottle with his trunk.

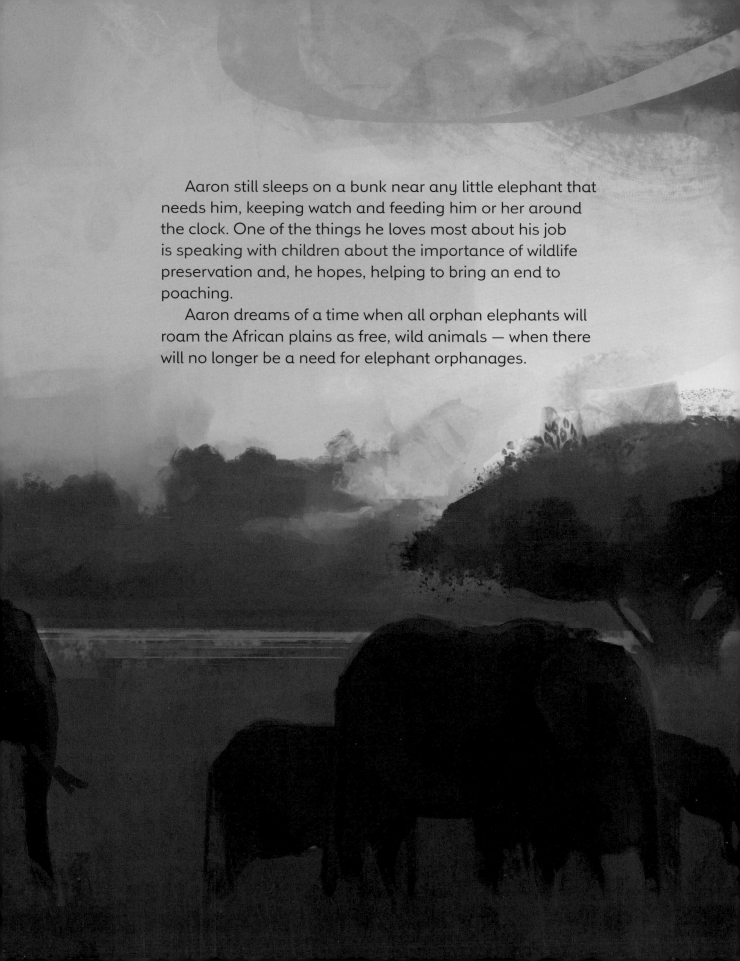

Aaron still sleeps on a bunk near any little elephant that needs him, keeping watch and feeding him or her around the clock. One of the things he loves most about his job is speaking with children about the importance of wildlife preservation and, he hopes, helping to bring an end to poaching.

Aaron dreams of a time when all orphan elephants will roam the African plains as free, wild animals — when there will no longer be a need for elephant orphanages.

The Elephant Orphanage Project

Run by Game Rangers International, a wildlife conservation NGO (non-governmental organization) in Zambia, the Elephant Orphanage Project specializes in the rescue and rehabilitation of orphaned elephants, with the long-term goal of reintroducing them into the wild.

Rescue, Rehabilitation, Release

The first stage is at the Lilayi Elephant Nursery, where the orphans undergo intensive care to treat dehydration, illness and wounds, as well as post-traumatic stress. Highly trained keepers stay with the elephants twenty-four hours a day to provide stability and help with recovery from the emotional damage the elephants have suffered from losing their families.

Very young baby elephants are bottle-fed a special formula and are cared for night and day. But as soon as possible, they also learn to browse in the surrounding forest.

The keepers take the elephants on walks to teach them which trees are edible, to train them to watch out for dangers and to help them learn other things about the environment that elephants would normally learn from their herds.

Elephants remain at the nursery until they no longer depend on milk and can survive mostly on an adult diet. This is usually when they are around three years old.

Once an elephant is ready, he or she is moved to the Kafue Release Facility. This facility is located inside Kafue National Park, the second largest park in Africa, and it borders an ancient teak forest where many wild elephants still roam. Here the orphans browse freely, surrounded by wilderness — although at night they remain in an area that is protected against predators until they are old enough and big enough to defend themselves, usually in their early teens. This is where they can meet wild elephants, learn to fend for themselves in the wild and to be accepted by wild herds again.

Meet Zambezi

There is a real Zambezi! He was only one month old when staff at a holiday lodge found him splashing around in their swimming pool. Severely dehydrated, the baby elephant had tried to drink from the pool and had fallen in. There was no sign of his mother or any other elephants. A team from the Elephant Orphanage Project and local conservation officers cared for the little elephant until he was stable enough to transport. Then he was flown to Lusaka to join other young elephants at the Lilayi Elephant Nursery, where he recovered physically and emotionally from the trauma of losing his mother and family. He was moved to the Kafue Release Facility in 2016, where he is gradually learning how to live in the wild.

Meet Aaron

This story is inspired by the real-life story of Aaron, one of the elephant keepers at the Lilayi Elephant Nursery. Aaron grew up in a village where hunting elephants was common, both as a way of protecting crops and to supply the ivory trade. Aaron had been brought up to see elephants as threatening animals. He says he will never forget the first time he saw humans and elephants interacting as friends. He thought there was witchcraft involved!

Aaron happened to be doing casual work for the local conservation organization that helped with Zambezi's rescue. Because of his natural ability to care for animals, Aaron was asked to help care for Zambezi during the two months before he could be moved to join the other orphans. Aaron was so good at his job that he was offered a full-time position at the Lilayi Elephant Nursery. He left his home on the banks of the Zambezi River to join Bezi at the nursery in Lusaka, where he has worked since 2012 and is now Team Leader of the elephant keepers.

How you can help

During my visit to the Lilayi Elephant Nursery, I learned how volunteers and various organizations make it possible to care for and release orphaned elephants. Here is how you, too, can help.

Adopt an elephant

You can reassure your parents that if you adopt an elephant, it won't come to live with you! But by making a donation, you will help all the elephants that are staying at the orphanage. Your donation helps to pay for milk, vitamins, medicine and much more. You will likely receive a photo and information about "your" elephant as well as regular updates. The following organizations run elephant adoption programs:

Game Rangers International is a conservation organization that works to protect wildlife in Zambia through several projects, including the Elephant Orphanage Project. http://www.gamerangersinternational.org

The David Sheldrick Wildlife Trust in Kenya runs one of the most successful orphan elephant rescue and rehabilitation programs in the world. The trust also rescues orphaned rhinos. https://www.sheldrickwildlifetrust.org

World Wildlife Fund has long been a world leader in wildlife conservation. Through the WWF, you can adopt not only elephants but also any other species at risk. http://www.worldwildlife.org

Get involved, donate or volunteer

There are many ways you can help protect elephants or other endangered animals and their habitats. Here are more organizations dedicated to protecting wildlife and the natural environment:

Game Rangers International operates a volunteer program each month. Volunteers can make a real difference, and can get involved in a variety of projects, including orphaned elephant observations, wildlife research, education and working with communities. http://www.gamerangersinternational.org

Roots & Shoots is a worldwide program based on the vision of Dr. Jane Goodall. You can participate in projects and activities, including protesting the use of ivory and educating others. Your class or school can get involved in many exciting projects and help by raising awareness or funds. http://www.rootsandshoots.org

The David Shepherd Wildlife Foundation works to protect critically endangered mammals in their wild habitat as well as benefit local communities that share their environment. The organization offers a number of ways to give your support. You can buy beautiful wildlife art or other gifts, donate money directly, fundraise, become a "friend," volunteer or adopt endangered animals. https://www.davidshepherd.org

Born Free is a nonprofit organization with offices in Africa, the United States and England whose mission is to end suffering of wild animals in captivity, rescue individual animals in need, protect wildlife in their natural habitats and encourage compassionate conservation globally. You can support this organization through any of its many programs, which include wildlife sponsorship and an online gift shop. http://www.bornfree.org.uk

World Wildlife Fund offers a number of ways to help besides its wildlife adoption program. You can also donate directly, become a member or get involved in a local chapter, and help by fundraising, learning about wildlife and spreading the word. http://www.worldwildlife.org

Glossary

boma: an enclosure, usually built in a circle, to protect huts and cattle from wildlife

dehydration: a harmful reduction of water in the body, which can be dangerous and even lead to death

foraging: searching for food, such as grasses, twigs and leaves

game ranger: a person who looks after and manages wildlife

hierarchy: a ranking system in which age and social bonds are important

Kanjani? (kahn-jah-nee): "How are you?" in Goba*

matriarch: the dominant female in a group, usually the oldest and most experienced

milk dependency: an infant animal's reliance on its mother's milk, or a special formula as substitute, for health and growth before it can eat solid foods only

Mwasela seyi (mwah-tsweh-lah say-ee): "Good afternoon" in Goba*

NGO: a non-governmental organization. Usually these are not-for-profit organizations, paying for their operating costs through donations and grants only.

nshima (nuh-SHEE-mah): a type of porridge or dough made from cornmeal

poaching: illegal hunting

post-traumatic stress: a mental health condition that can occur after experiencing shock, and which can lead to depression and anxiety

weaning: the period during which the infant switches slowly from drinking only milk to including solids and finally not needing milk anymore

***Goba** is one of many languages spoken in Zambia. It is the language Aaron, who is from the Lower Zambezi region, speaks.

◆ ◆ ◆

Acknowledgments

This book was inspired by my visit
to the Lilayi Elephant Nursery in Zambia. The staff of Game
Rangers International, who run this facility as well as the release
facilities in Kafue National Park, and the staff at the David Shepherd
Wildlife Foundation, which funds and supports the projects, have all
been very helpful during my research and were very welcoming.

Thank you to Aaron and the other gamekeepers for
the amazing work you do! Thank you to Rachel Murton for all your
patient fact-checking. A special thank you to my editor, Yasemin
Uçar, for your vision and persistence in getting the story just right.
And to Pedro ... for showing Zambia just as I saw it.